ALEC GUINNESS

by Kenneth Tynan

Angus McBea

Hamlet—1951

Alec Guinness

by

KENNETH TYNAN

An illustrated study of his work for stage and screen, with a list of his appearances

SALISBURY SQUARE · LONDON

Printed in Great Britain by
The Camelot Press Ltd., London and Southampton

CONTENTS

ILLUSTRATIONS

"When you think you have him,
eel-like, he eludes your grasp."

ALEC GUINNESS, as Shaw once observed of Irving, has no face. You notice it—or rather, fail to notice it—as soon as he enters a room. Jeeves-fashion, he shimmers in and is amongst you: a slight man, balding and bland, with deprecating, sloped shoulders which he shrugs constantly. And above the shoulders—"A blank, my lord", impassive as an almond. From it, if occasion warrants, a caressing snicker may emerge, accompanied by a rakish tilt of the head and a twitch of a smile, resembling the crescent moon. You might easily take him for a slightly tipsy monk, unfrocked for giggling in confession. By staring hard, you may assure yourself that he has eyes: superficially guileless, they are in truth sly and wary, and, rather than meet your gaze, they will wander contemplatively from side to side, avoiding contact like a magnet pushed close to another of like pole. As you watch them, noting how pale and glazed they are, you find you have forgotten the face; and vice versa. The whole presence of the man is guarded and evasive. Slippery sums him up; when you think you have him, eel-like, he eludes your grasp. Should you try to pluck out the heart of his mystery, he grows cautious; he will communicate intimacy, but always from a considerable distance, as if through a reversed telescope. The philosophers of Locke's school held that the mind of a child was an unmarked slate, on which passions and circumstances left their casual trace: so with the phizz of Guinness. He looks unmemorable. Were he to commit a murder, I have no doubt that the number of false arrests following the circulation of his description would break all records.

His facelessness, then, is quite different from Irving's. The mere sight of Irving, strolling along Grafton Street, was enough to convince anyone that here was not only an actor, but a famous one. The average man's idea of an actor is still not far removed from that of Mr. Partridge in *Tom Jones*, who was taken to see Garrick in *Hamlet*, which impressed him mightily; and yet . . . he liked the King, when all was done, better than the Prince, because, as he put it: "He speaks all his words distinctly, half as loud again as the other. —Any Body may see he is an Actor." G. H. Lewes, a century later, examined Partridge's opinion and decided that he agreed with it. Garrick's Hamlet might have been, as Partridge allowed, "natural": but "it is obvious," in Lewes' judgment, "that the naturalness required from Hamlet is very different from the naturalness of a Partridge." In other words, the simulation of Hamlet, or of any rhetorical hero, any "ideal character", has little to do with the simulation of life. In this piece of dramatic theory, the eighteenth and nineteenth centuries join hands.

And Guinness, meanwhile, is left out: neither Partridge nor Lewes, one is sure, would have sympathised very strongly with him. Acting, when he is about a Stage, loses its capital A—a tall, commanding symbol, appropriately astride. The admirers of John Philip Kemble would probably have found much to commend in John Gielgud; and Olivier, had he lived a century and a half ago, might well have set up in opposition to Edmund Kean. But Guinness is a prodigy, belonging to no tradition. He is tethered to his own epoch. He embodies, as does no one else, a modern-dress manner of acting, neither classic nor romantic, into which the doubt, the indecision, and even the cynicism of the twentieth century have all been craftily assimilated. When Guinness affects *le style noble*, it is usually for purposes of satire. It sits awkwardly on him, and he tends to chuckle at it.

"Great acting": along with the phrase there troop into one's mind Salvini, Bernhardt, Rachel, Irving. At the core of talents like these, there is a strong, personal turbulence. At the core of Guinness' impersonations there is a kind of impersonal peace. He is a master, but a master of anonymity; only the

Picture Post Library

Guinness at home

Picture Post Librar

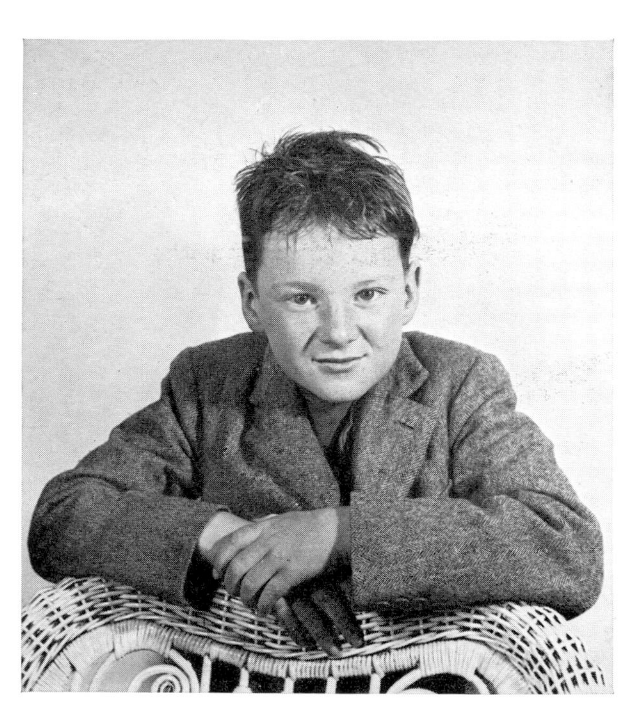

With Merula, his wife, an
Matthew

Picture Post Library

Mander & Mitchenson Collection

His first appearance on the stage: as a Junior Counsel in *Libel!* (1934)

1. Aubrey Mather
2. Malcolm Keen
3. Frances Doble
4. Basil Dignam
5. Beckett Bould
6. Anthony Hollis
7. Leon M. Lion
8. Sir Nigel Playfair
9. Michael Barry
10. Joe Mitchenson
11. Alec Guinness
12. Mark Dignum
13. Twigge Molecey
14. John Stewart Bingley

elect pierce to his soul; to the rest he is a cipher, a judicious and unbroken code. His obsequious magic gets its results not by noise or declamation, but—almost—by spells. He has banished from his artistic vocabulary what Hazlitt would have called "the striking effect". Apply Guinness' technique to drawing-room comedy, and it seems unremarkable; but import it, as he does, into rhetorical drama, and at once it is as refreshing as a revolution. It is also inimitable. Springing from no tradition, Guinness will likewise create none. He exists in a histrionic air-pocket, isolated and circumscribed by his own eccentricity. Max Beerbohm says somewhere that he always thought of Irving as "The Knight from Nowhere", a title which, with one emendation, might now pass to Guinness. The emendation is in the direction of whimsey. "The White Knight", let us say, "from Nowhere."

His real origins are not quite as obscure as that. Not from nowhere he came, but from Maida Vale in London, where he was born on 2nd April, 1914. There was little money in the family, and Guinness left school at fifteen to seek employment, which he found as junior copywriter in an advertising agency. Here he spent eighteen months of alternate incompetence and inertia. "My career in advertising ended," he explains, "when I mistakenly ordered a four-foot half-tone engraving instead of a four-inch one, as I was supposed to." Already he was enlivening his spare time with weekly visits to the gallery of the Old Vic. A solitary, unclubbable youth, he was easily bruised and flustered by the demands of ordinary social intercourse, preferring silent communion with the richly articulate people of the theatre, whose public appearances were rehearsed and perfect. This was less trouble, and more rewarding. He, hidden in a darkened auditorium: they, disguised beneath make-up and other men's words—an ideal relationship. In most art there is an element of showing-off: was there, in Guinness' devotion to the theatre, an element of compensation for imagined inadequacies? It is possible. Many people have entered the profession for worse reasons.

While he was still technically a trainee in advertising, Guinness began to take lessons in acting from Martita Hunt, then, in the early thirties, at the height of her erratic powers.

At first she assumed that he was a member of the brewing family: as gently as he could, he corrected her. She took the news on the chin, but discouragement set in shortly afterwards, and, at the end of a dozen sessions, she peered into a very fallible crystal ball and announced to Guinness that he would never make an actor. Defiantly, he entered for and won a scholarship to the now defunct Fay Compton Studio of Dramatic Art. During his first term he, along with several fellow-students, obtained a walk-on part in *Libel!*, Edward Wooll's court-room drama at the Playhouse. Here, as a speechless junior counsel, he made his stage debut on 2nd April, 1934—his twentieth birthday. His salary, twelve shillings a week, formed the greater part of his total income. At the Studio's Public Show, an annual matinée, he recited a snippet of Mercutio, sang "Waiting at the Gate for Katie", and dominated a mime play, devised by Compton Mackenzie, about the proprietor of a Punch-and-Judy stand who beat his wife to death. The judges, one of whom was John Gielgud, gave him the first prize, a leather-bound Shakespeare. Unable to afford further tuition, he left the school next day. He had half-a-crown in his pocket, and looked even less like an actor than he does now.

For a while his quondam colleagues at the Studio helped to keep him, barely subsisting, in a grubby Bayswater attic. Repeatedly he bearded Gielgud, his benefactor, who remarked on one such occasion: "You're far too thin", and offered a loan of twenty pounds. Guinness turned it down as brightly as possible, and kicked himself all the way home. In August, 1934, he managed to land his first speaking part—or parts, for in Noel Langley's *Queer Cargo* he played, with prophetic versatility, a Chinese coolie (Act I), a French pirate (Act II), and a British matelot (Act III). He continued, when matinées permitted, to go to the Old Vic. Scanning the audience at a performance of *Richard II* one afternoon, he saw Gielgud and made a mental note to bump into him afterwards—needlessly, as it happened, because Gielgud strode up to him, wasting no time on greetings, and invited him to play Osric in his forthcoming *Hamlet* at the New Theatre. Swaying a little, Guinness agreed, thereby accepting the shelter of a large wing

Bertram Park

In John Gielgud's 1934 *Hamlet*. Above: as Third Player (4th from left).
Below: as Osric (3rd from right)

Bertram Park

A. Consol

Wolf (2nd from left) in *Noah*. Prone in the foreground is Merula Salaman, who played Tiger

Howard Coster

Bertram Park

Romeo and Juliet (1935). Left: as Sampson (centre, in background). Right: as the Apothecary (with John Gielgud)

Houston Rogers

Yakov, drawing the curtains in *The Seagull*

J. W. Debenham *By courtesy of the Vic-Wells Association*

William (5th from right) in *As You Like It*

J. W. Debenham

Boyet, with beard and moustache, in *Love's Labour's Lost*

J. W. Debenha

Hamlet (1937): Robert Newton, Laurence Olivier, and Guinness (Osric)

J. W. Debenham

Andrew Aguecheek in *Twelfth Night*, with Laurence Olivier as Toby Belch

J. W. Debenh

Exeter in *Henry V*: with Laurence Olivier and Harcourt Williams

from which, psychologically, he later found it hard to escape. Since that day he has never been unemployed, except by his own choice, for more than a month at a time; and he has always, apart from tours, special engagements and overseas trips, worked in London. Guinness is the only English player of the first rank who owes nothing at all to provincial repertory. His talent, a diamond pencil, addressed its subtle tracings directly to metropolitan taste; and, to a certain extent, still does so. His name, talismanic in London, carries much less weight north of the Trent.

In *Hamlet*, which ran for 155 performances, he doubled Osric and the Third Player for seven pounds a week. He has a natural bent for playing waterflies, and his Osric charmed most of the critics: "an admirable popinjay", Ivor Brown called it, "and wisely not effeminate." Your traditional star actor is lost when not playing leads; Guinness has sometimes looked lost when not playing supporting parts—in which, incredibly, he has never received a bad notice. He spent two years supporting Gielgud in *Hamlet*, Obey's *Noah, Romeo and Juliet* and *The Seagull*, during which time two strong, shaping influences were at work on him: that of Michel Saint-Denis and, more irresistible, that of Gielgud himself. Saint-Denis, a deep-burrowing mole in the mountain of Stanislavsky, did not make much impression on Guinness, an instinctive actor if ever there was one; but Gielgud he adored as a great ringmaster and a fanatical, if somewhat cowing trainer. Here, in full cry, was the last representative in England of the romantic tradition, with all its anguished disciplines and its stringent emphasis on "style". Gielgud may have made his pupil self-conscious—he stiffened many young actors with his exactions—but with him, sponge-like under Niagara, Guinness stayed until the summer of 1936.

Then began a long period of shuttling, which lasted until the outbreak of war, between Gielgud, the actor's actor, and Tyrone Guthrie, the producer's producer, then in command at the Old Vic. A surprisingly large number of Guinness' best parts come under two headings, courtiers and simpletons, and his first season at Waterloo Road contained specimens of both. Boyet in *Love's Labour's Lost* was his trial canter, followed by William in *As You Like It*, a performance which Alan Dent described as "a wondrous blank". In Laurence Olivier's *Hamlet* he played Reynaldo and Osric, and understudied the lead; but the part which first lifted him a notch above the supernumeraries was Andrew Aguecheek in Guthrie's production of *Twelfth Night*. This was singled out as a collector's item, and no fewer than three overnight reviews mentioned the similarity, often noticed since, between Guinness and Stan Laurel—the pale, mooncalf eyes, the dipping mop of fair hair, and the tituppy, loose-armed walk. One critic suggested that with this Sir Andrew, Oliver Hardy would make the perfect Toby Belch.

The 1937–8 season, a happy and memorable one, whisked Guinness back to Gielgud, now in residence at the Queen's Theatre. This was the time of Gielgud's definitive *Richard II*: Guinness played Aumerle and the royal groom, and afterwards, with a veritable *canule* of a putty nose, Snake in *The School for Scandal*. As Fedotik, he was intermittently visible in the classic Saint-Denis production of *The Three Sisters*; and he crowned the season with a performance of Lorenzo in *The Merchant of Venice* which touched with bliss the normally inscrutable features of Ivor Brown: Guinness, he wrote, "lifts the final scene to an unspectacular, meditative, star-struck beauty that takes the breath away." The romantic roles in Guinness' career are few in number; amorous ecstasy is something to which his nature does not readily surrender; and his success as Lorenzo must always be something of a marvel to those who (like myself) did not see it. Perhaps one should invoke the personal heresy, and recall that a few months later, in the summer of 1938, he married a friendly, freckled, ginger-haired actress named Merula Salaman, whom he had met three years before in *Noah*.

Like nearly everyone who witnessed it, he had been profoundly stirred by the performance of the American actress Carol Goodner as Masha in *The Three Sisters*, and he was accordingly overjoyed when asked to play opposite her in *The Doctor's Dilemma* for a couple of weeks in June. This was a significant interlude, largely because of the part's curious aptness to Guinness' capabilities. Shaw has confronted the

Houston Rogers

Aumerle (extreme right) in Gielgud's *Richard II*

Houston Rog

Snake in *The School for Scandal*, with Dorothy Green and Merula Salaman

Houston Rogers

Above (extreme right) and below: Fedotik in *The Three Sisters*

Houston Rog

Lorenzo in *The Merchant of Venice* (with Genevieve Jessel)

actor playing Louis Dubedat with several appalling problems: the man is a die-hard eccentric, his life a series of petty impostures, yet we must never for a moment doubt that he is a painter of genius. Now Guinness is an actor with a unique flair for eccentricity, a love of minor imposture, and, more than these, an ability (still not fully exploited) to imply the presence of genius in the characters he plays. To this we shall be returning: as a simple mnemonic, let me point out that Guinness is all but an anagram of geniuses. Dubedat, more than any other part he had played, foreshadowed his career in miniature, and one would like to see him in it again.

By mid-1938 he had appeared in four productions by Gielgud and six by Guthrie, whose approach was the precise antithesis of Gielgud's. It offered freedom and elbow-room, relaxation and abandon. Guthrie's actors were unjabbed by any spur save the spur of the moment: a mischievous improvisation was the keynote of his method, and through his productions, along with brilliant ingenuity, there gambolled a sort of inspired carelessness. Guinness went back to Guthrie and the Vic in September. The season opened quietly with *Trelawny of the "Wells"*; and then, in October, its centre-piece was unveiled, Guthrie's modern-dress *Hamlet*, with Guinness in the lead. The production bestowed on his name an aura of civilised controversy which it has never quite lost.

Guthrie described his new *Hamlet* as a cadenza "on the familiar theme of the Painted Smile and the Breaking Heart". Visually, it was much more than that: the costumes, deliberately startling, included lounge suits, flannels, trilbies and (for the graveyard scene) a seaman's jersey and gumboots. It was well and in some quarters joyously received; and Guinness' performance, the prelude to his maturity as an actor, was entirely symbolic of his capacities. Of its clarity, sensitivity and magnetism there were few doubts; but it had plenty of deficiencies. It lacked power; it lacked what Agate used to call "magnoperation"; and it refused, as Agate said, to attempt the ABC of the part. Possessing chubby, practical hands, Guinness attempted few rhetorical gestures; himself unflamboyant, he eschewed conventional flourishes; the whole performance, in short, marked his independence of the past.

Agate put the case best when he wrote (the italics are his) that Guinness' Hamlet failed "*because it deliberately refuses to succeed.* This young actor . . . attempts neither play of feature nor gesture. He rejects mordancy. He puts no scorn into 'this quintessence of dust'. He gabbles, making reply before he has time to take in the thing provoking the reply. . . . Yet this non-acting comes, in the end, to have a value of its own." Agate conceded that Guinness played the last scene, after Osric's departure, better than any other Hamlet he had seen. But the "non-acting" which worried him so was in fact Guinness' secretive style, in bud, but not yet in flower. Having discarded the positive virtues of costume rhetoric, he had little, as yet, with which to replace them; little beyond finesse, hatred of excess, and innate pathos. For the huntsman's arrow he substituted the embroiderer's needle; but at twenty-four he was not quite capable of a great design. His Hamlet was a performance compounded of all his defects, polished until they shone.

He must some day try another modern-dress Hamlet. I saw one last year, and it reminded me powerfully of Kafka: the central character emerged as a lonely young man, burdened with an unsought and unwelcome mission, which he was unable to carry out because of the intervention of mysterious and delusive obstacles. The palace was presented as a stronghold of bureaucracy, with grey-clad minions scurrying to and fro on meaningless errands: and there, dazed in their midst, was Hamlet, with a murder to perform. When actors wear doublet and hose and pronounce the lines with "stylish" uniformity, one's ears become deaf to their precise meaning; but in modern dress one fact obtrudes. Apart from Claudius, a short-lived penitent in the prayer scene, Hamlet is the only person in the play who cares about God. He doubts the provenance of the ghost—is it from hell or heaven? He will not kill the King until his heels may "kick at heaven"; having seen the ghost, he'll "go pray"; he would dispatch Ophelia to a nunnery; he swears "by the rood" and reflects that man is "in apprehension, how like a god!"; he talks of the abuse of "god-like reason" and envisages himself as heaven's "scourge and minister"; he enjoins Gertrude to confess herself to heaven;

and it is not just by formal chance that Horatio invokes flights of angels to sing him to his rest. And when Laertes returns, sword in hand, to avenge his own father's murder, the contrast between the two men is violent and immediate. "I dare damnation", shouts Laertes; and we are at once reminded that Hamlet's tragedy is that he cannot dare damnation, cannot bring himself to perform an act unsanctioned by heaven. I suspect that Guinness, an actor who specialises in men with obsessions, might be able to emphasise this religious melancholy more tellingly than anyone else: and mention of Kafka prompts me to regret the fact that he did not play K. in the stage version of *The Trial*.

After *Hamlet*, he appeared as Bob Acres in Guthrie's production of *The Rivals*: again he denied tradition, fought shy of the hearty buffoon, and gave a much shyer, feyer reading of the part. That winter he saw the signposts—Gielgud pointing one way, towards stylised glory, and Guthrie another, towards conscious waywardness. He took stock and, offending nobody, sought to elude their shadows by carving out a separate path for himself.

The next year, 1939, was a full one. Guinness toured the Continent and Egypt with the Vic, and then, in June, returned to the Waterloo Road in a revival, directed by Rupert Doone, of Auden and Isherwood's *The Ascent of F.6*, which had been originally produced two years before by the Group Theatre. The theme of genius recurred. Guinness told an interviewer that he had been drawn to the play because Ransom, its protagonist, was modelled in part on T. E. Lawrence, one of his heroes. To aspire, to risk, to achieve dangerously: these had fired him. One of the more unexpected facets of his personality is the fascination held for him by explorers, leaders and warriors: he would dearly love to play Captain Cook or General Wolfe. W. A. Darlington wrote of him in *The Ascent of F.6*: "Alec Guinness brings to the playing of Michael Ransom . . . a sense of the concentration and integrity that belong to genius." That review must have pleased him as much as any he has ever received.

In July he accepted an invitation to play Romeo at the Scottish Theatre Festival in Perth. It was, he now admits, a mistake: and certainly it is tricky to conceive of Guinness in the grip of Romeo's passion. Back in London, he completed a project long in mind, a stage adaptation of *Great Expectations,* which George Devine directed at the Rudolf Steiner Hall. With unbounded gaiety and élan, Guinness played Herbert Pocket, Pip's room-mate and confidant, a performance which he later reproduced in the screen version of the novel. He has done nothing quite like it, nothing quite so ebullient, dashing and open-hearted. Two less triumphant engagements followed—with Edith Evans in *Cousin Muriel,* Clemence Dane's comedy about kleptomania, and with Gielgud in *The Tempest* at the Old Vic.

During the first summer of the war he toured the country in the highly appropriate role of Charleston in *Thunder Rock.* Charleston is a man with a closed heart: here, as in many of his subsequent successes, Guinness played a character cut-off, benighted and sequestered, an intransigent member of Stendhal's "les Happy Few". The part had been created in London by Michael Redgrave, another actor beloved of solitariness, who prefers, one might say, islands on stage to peninsulas. Both Redgrave and Guinness have since been forced to adjust their natural isolation to the playgoer's insatiable demand for intimacy: the stage, after all, is not a laboratory. Redgrave, in a sincere effort to make his involved mental processes explicable to an average audience, adopted an intensely graphic, slightly algebraic style of acting which confused his admirers as often as it illuminated them; unwilling to compromise with minds less subtle than his own, he took on the mantle of a lecturer attempting to popularise without cheapness the mysteries of nuclear fission. Guinness, as chary as Redgrave of direct emotional statement, found another answer. Rather than expose himself, he hooded himself yet more raptly; became still more remote; developed, in fact, into a kind of sympathetic enigma.

In 1941 he joined the Navy as an ordinary seaman. Within twelve months he gained a commission, and spent much of the war ferrying butter and hay to the Yugoslavs. Quite by chance, he was the first man ashore in the invasion of Sicily. Unknown to him, the time of the landing had been

J. W. Debenham

Arthur Gower in *Trelawny of the 'Wells'* (with Sophie Stewart and O. B. Clarence)

Anth

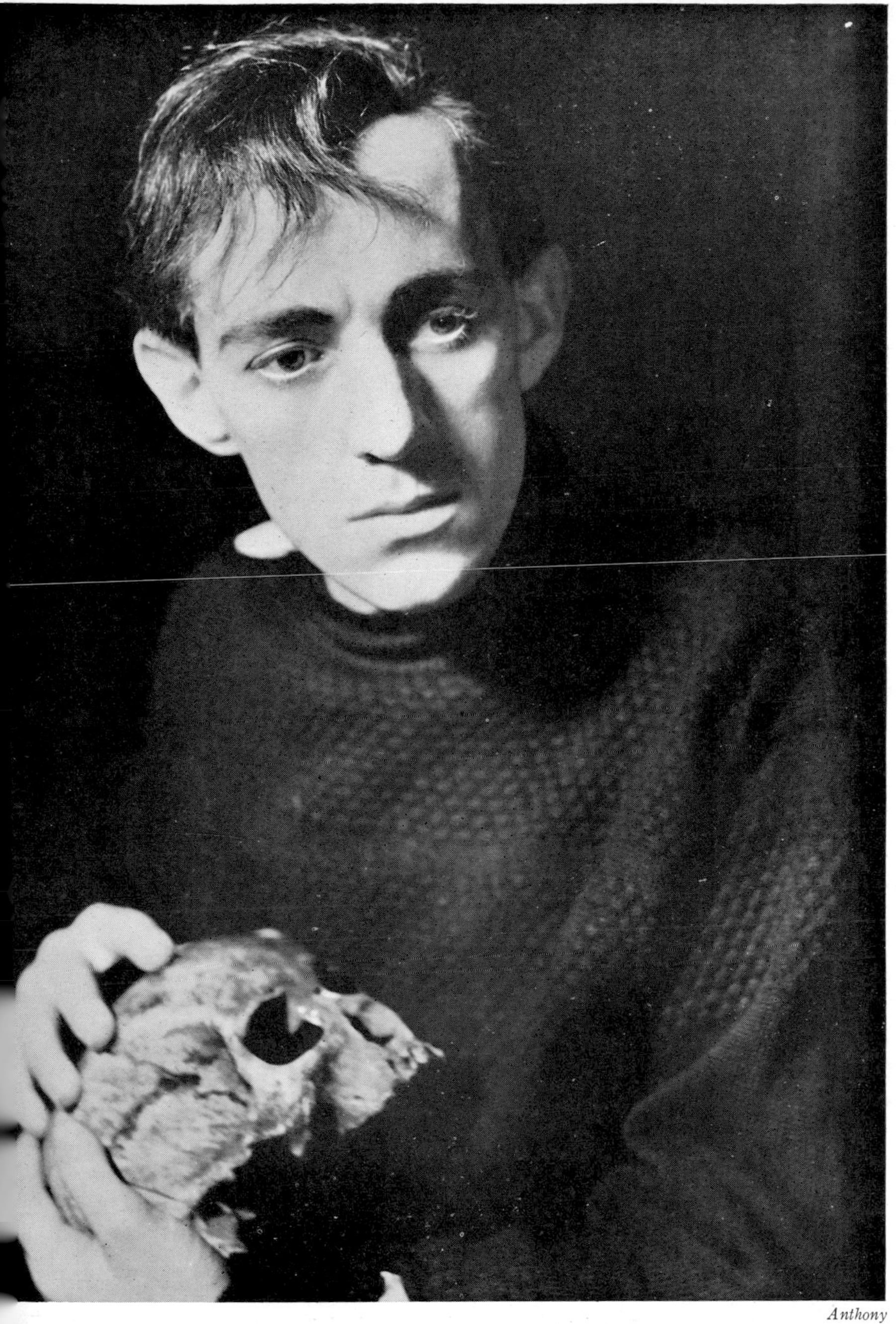

Anthony

Hamlet in modern dress—1938

·ft: with Hermione Hannen (Ophelia)

Anth

Hamlet with the Ghost (Malcolm Keen)

postponed, and he arrived at the beach, lonely at the helm of a landing-craft, an hour early. Later, with understandable petulance, he greeted the admiral with the curt but ill-advised assertion that such tardiness would never—*never*—be tolerated in the West End theatre.

He returned to the stage in 1946, playing Mitya in his own adaptation of *The Brothers Karamazov*, which was ferociously directed by Peter Brook at the Lyric, Hammersmith. Testily munching his nails, he played Mitya as a prolonged *crise de nerfs*, a scorn-darting recluse, and was beaten to the notices by the lousy, life-hugging patriarch which Frederick Valk made of old Karamazov. A month later, he removed his *toupet* and summed up the shame of France as Garcin, the disgraced cynic, in Brook's production of *Huis Clos* at the Arts Theatre, an event which connoisseurs from both sides of the Atlantic flocked briskly to see. By now Guinness' name was known, and offers from America were plentiful. He turned them down to rejoin the Old Vic, which had then reached a turning-point in its history. The two great Olivier-Richardson seasons, 1944–5 and 1945–6, the seasons of *Richard III*, the two parts of *Henry IV*, and *Oedipus*, were over. Richardson was to stay for another winter, but Olivier's Lear, self-directed in September, 1946, was his farewell to the Vic. In these giant footsteps Guinness was groomed to follow.

His first year did not take him far outside his usual range, courtiers and simpletons. First, the Fool in *Lear*, whom he presented as a bereft little fellow with a vein of mordant cruelty in him, rejoicing in his shafts of wit even as he watched his master impaled on them. "Sad, bilious loyalty" was Philip Hope-Wallace's phrase, and a just one. Next, a feeble, good-hearted rip in Priestley's *An Inspector Calls*; and then, an icily stylish De Guiche in Guthrie's production of *Cyrano de Bergerac*.

It was not until *The Alchemist*, the last play of the season, that Guinness gave a performance worthy of his promise. He played Abel Drugger, Garrick's old part; and though he cannot have known how Garrick played it, he made it clear why Garrick played it. Drugger is the innocent young tobacconist with cheese-tainted breath, who brings gifts to Face, the alchemist's tout, as to a shrine. I wrote at the time:

> "Mr. Guinness manages to get to the heart of all good, hopeful young men who can enjoy without envy the company of wits. . . . His face creases ruddily into modest delight, and he stamps his thin feet in glee. In a later scene, he demonstrates a very rare gift, that of suggesting the change that comes over a man when he is alone. Drugger is commissioned by Face to bring him a Spanish costume as disguise. He trots away and returns, shyly clad in its showy cloak and hat. Waiting for Face to answer the door, he begins to execute timid dance-steps under the porch. He treads a rapt, self-absorbed measure with himself, consumed with joy. Then Face appears: the pretence is over, he recognises his intellectual master, and, not regretfully or pathetically, but smartly and prosaically, he sheds his costume and hands it over."

This was a first glimpse of Guinness' quiddity, and of part of the secret of his magnetism. He can seem unobserved: he can make every member of the audience an eavesdropper on a private ceremonial. His art is the art of public solitude.

The 1947–8 Old Vic season began ambitiously with *Richard II*, a part bigger than any which had come Guinness' way since Hamlet, nine years before. A tentative and unassuming man, he approached the producer, Ralph Richardson, before rehearsals began, to find out what kind of a Richard he might have in mind. Richardson, an overwhelmingly cryptic conversationalist, looked up at Guinness, his face clouding into a sort of oppressed vagueness, and said: "I'll tell you, old fellow." He picked up a lead pencil, worn and shiny, and waved it about. "Like that. Sharp and slim. That's what we want." On this basis the play went into production. The result, for me, was a disappointment. In the bits which we knew he could play, Guinness used none but familiar devices; and in the rest, of which we were doubtful, he uncovered nothing new. Either he or his producer failed to show us the "rash, fierce blaze of riot" which Gaunt indicts—and which,

Right: Bob Acres in *The Rivals*

J. W. Debenham

News Chronicle

Michael Ransom in *The Ascent of F.6*, with (L. to R.) Frederick Peisley, Arthur Macrae, Laurier Lister, and Ernest Hare

Romeo and Juliet (1939, at Perth): Guinness and Pamela Stanley

Angus McB[illegible]

Richard Meilhac in *Cousin Muriel*, with Edith Evans

Edwin Smith

Ferdinand (right) in *The Tempest*, with John Gielgud and Marius Goring

Vandamm Stud

Flight-Lieutenant Graham in *Flare Path* (New York)

Angus McBean

Mitya in *The Brothers Karamazov*, with Pierre Lefevre

John Vick

Garcin in *Vicious Circle* (*Huis Clos*): in the background, Beatrix Lehmann and Betty Ann Davies

it must be admitted, no Richard has ever shown us. He was best in the deposition scene. Here Richard was not only disdainful; he was almost ashamed of the hypersensitivity which forbade him to come to terms with the brutish power-politicians who would make off with his birth-right. His delivery of the crown to Bolingbroke was a masterpiece of delicate scorn. With a freezing smile, he dangled the golden round an inch from the usurper's nose, and gave an entrancing overtone of sarcasm to: "Here cousin, *seize* the crown." He was fine, too, in the first-act quarrel between Norfolk and Bolingbroke. As the gloves hurtled across the stage and the row ripened, Richard sat impassive and patently bored, occasionally stroking, with dandyish detachment, the beginnings of a beard. But these were but glimmers of the Richard we had expected. The production encouraged Guinness to attempt too many big vocal effects: it set him speaking at the top of his voice, a meandering tenor which has no top at all. Occasionally, in a few razor-edged moments, he equalled the best that had been done with the part: and in the deposition scene he rightly called to mind Henry James' phrase about "a Bohemian wanting tremendously to be a Philistine".

Lionel Birch in *Picture Post* wrote interestingly:

> "Guinness' conception of Richard of Bordeaux was of a man always capable of standing . . . a little apart from himself and looking at himself. The man outside observing the man within—but both men resident in different worlds. Private worlds indicated by private jokes which started at the corners of Guinness' mouth. . . . Some people might find this interpretation too cynical and insufficiently 'poetical' for their pre-conceptions. To me it seemed the true apocalyptic link between this cat-and-mouse king's tweaks of sadism at the beginning of the play and his twists of masochism at the end of it."

This is a skilful piece of pleading, in which I detect an element of rationalisation. What Birch describes as "Guinness' conception of Richard of Bordeaux" is in reality Guinness' conception of any protagonist under forty. There are private worlds and private jokes in any number of his performances: it is, in fact, a fair criticism of his technique that it encourages him to act like that, detaching himself from the character instead of investing himself in it. The theatre, unlike the grave, is a fine and public place, and audiences have a way of growing impatient with an actor who will not trust them with his secrets. If Birch's exegesis is correct, and that was indeed Guinness' interpretation, then he was, in poker parlance, playing it very close to the table.

A neat courtier-cum-simpleton followed: the Dauphin in *Saint Joan*, with Celia Johnson as the incinerated *franc-tireuse*. Once more, the critics spotted the likeness to Stan Laurel and commended the mastery of make-up: but Peter Ustinov had the most evocative phrase for Guinness' performance, which he summed up as "one of those walking pear-drops he does so well". The third play was Gogol's *The Government Inspector*, in which Guinness, as the upstart Hlestakov, developed a hint he had dropped a few months earlier in the solo fandango of Abel Drugger. Hlestakov, like Drugger in Face's cloak, is a little man drapped in finery not his own, which he is determined to enjoy while he may, and Guinness carried off the imposture with a wonderfully cool and canny *panache*. He was most praised, though, for his display in the next and last production of the season, *Coriolanus*, with John Clements in the title-role. Menenius, Guinness' part, is the patrician peace-maker who is sandwiched between Coriolanus, the Junker-militarist, and the rude, obstreperous plebs: this is a play of three estates, not (as the textbooks say) two. Guinness beautifully conveyed the finesse beneath the old senator's fumbling, and ran away with most of the reviews. Nowadays most people take it for granted that his *expertise* in assuming old age comes of long practice: but the fact is that, unless we count the last scene of *Saint Joan*, Menenius in May, 1948, was the first veteran leading role he had ever played on the stage.

He had begun to make successful advances to wider audiences. The casual ease of his style suited the close-up camera, which recoils as if stung from rhetoric. In his first film, *Great Expectations*, which appeared in 1946, he repeated his buoyant stage

John Vickers

Eric Birling in *An Inspector Calls*, with Margaret Leighton

The Fool in Laurence Olivier's
King Lear

John Vickers

John Vickers

John Vi

De Guiche in *Cyrano de Bergerac*, with Nicholas Hannen and John Arnold

John Vickers

Drugger's entrance in *The Alchemist*

John Vicke

Abel Drugger in *The Alchemist*

John Vickers

Menenius Agrippa in *Coriolanus*

John Vick

Richard II (1947): Above, in Act I. Right, in Act V

John Vickers

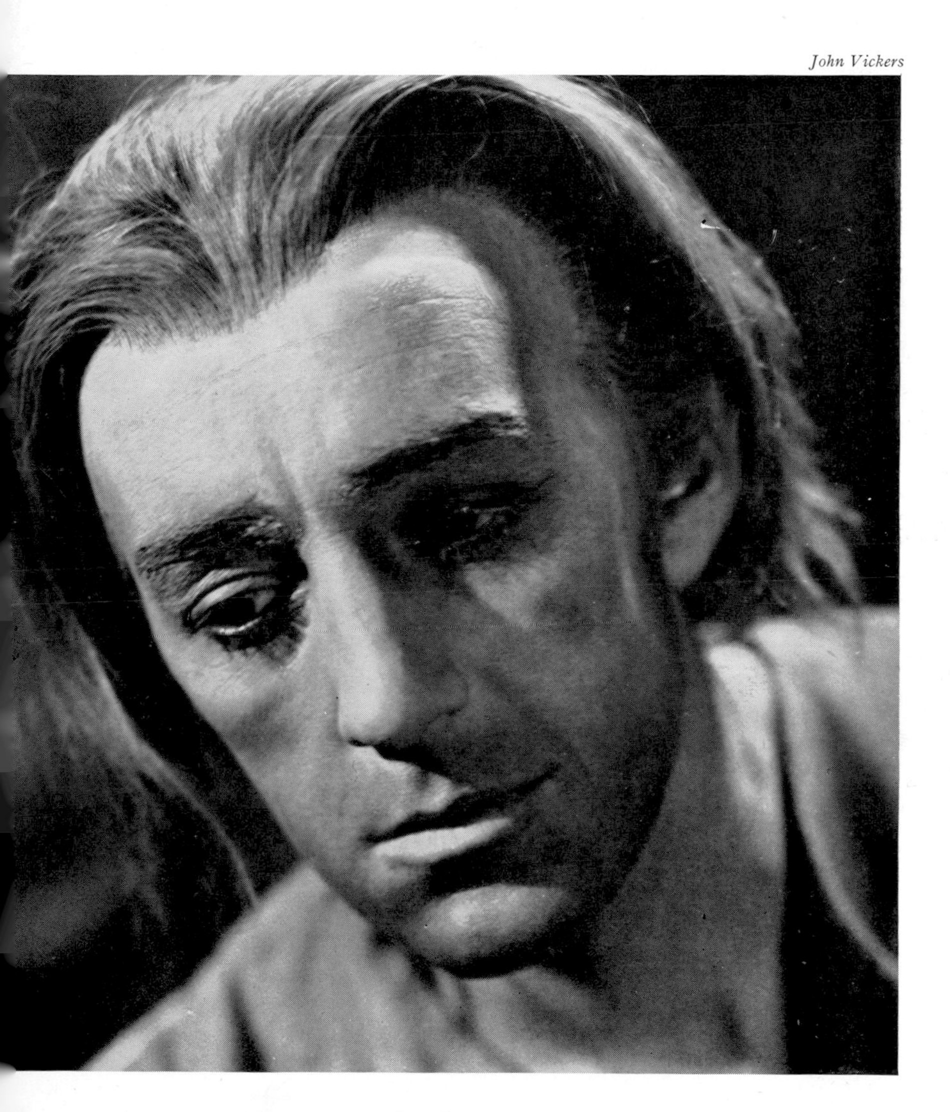

John Vick

The Dauphin in *Saint Joan* (with Celia Johnson)

John Vickers

The Dauphin in the Epilogue

John Vick

Hlestakov in *The Government Inspector*

performance of Herbert Pocket: his second, *Oliver Twist* (1948) was also directed by David Lean for Cineguild, and Guinness made a grim but not unlikeable Fagin, replete with Punch-like *gouaillerie*. What drew him so fruitfully to Dickens was probably his penchant for the uncommon man, the man who is content with and reconciled to his own oddities. He who lives happily with his quirks is a comic character; he who fears or despises them is a figure of pathos, even of tragedy. It was the former sort which attracted Guinness. James Agate once said that if *Dombey and Son* were to be adapted for the stage, Guinness would be the ideal Mr. Toots; and many other Dickensian characters are well within his grasp.

Popular actors rarely resist the temptation to become directors. In the autumn of 1948 Guinness yielded to it: he produced *Twelfth Night* for the Old Vic, but in untoward circumstances, because the casting and scenery were bespoken before he was called in, and neither proved to be satisfactory. Feste was elevated to the status of hero. He became an omniscient observer, a shrewd and wintry oddling—in short, a Guinness creation. Robert Eddison, who played the part, looked like a consumptive prince in exile: at his waist he carried a drum, on which he frequently beat little tattoos of despair, as well he might, for the piece was so interpreted that he was in love with Olivia and fully aware that Cesario was really Viola. All this, of course, simply added another leading character to a play which has too many to begin with. Cedric Hardwicke's soldierly Sir Toby, a cashiered Blimp, came superbly to the rescue: delectably bloodshot and rumpled, this was the best Belch I have ever seen. The production was Guinness' swan-song at the Vic. When he left, the company's reputation dimmed, and there were few signs of renaissance until *Romeo and Juliet*, four years later.

Feeling that a frontal assault on the commercial theatre had now become imperative, Guinness went into *The Human Touch*, which was produced at the Savoy in February, 1949. In this simple, anti-obscurantist tract, he played Dr. James Simpson of Edinburgh, who pioneered the anaesthetic use of chloroform in the middle years of the last century. It was greeted with respectful yawns and ran on Guinness' name for 113 performances. Thereafter, he absented himself from the London stage for two years. Films occupied much of his time. He made two in 1949: the second, *A Run for Your Money*, in which he was a gardening correspondent trying feebly to be a star reporter, was no match for the first, *Kind Hearts and Coronets*—Robert Hamer's masterpiece, and the climax of Guinness' screen career. One of John Gielgud's proudest memories is of his mother's appearance at Ellen Terry's jubilee performance: in Act I of *Much Ado About Nothing*, twenty-three parts were played by various members of the Terry family. In Hamer's stylish murdering-piece, Guinness set up a new individual record: eight speaking parts, one non-speaking cameo and a portrait in oils were played by the same member of the Guinness family. No other English film has approached *Kind Hearts* in the matter of period wit; and in the French cinema, only *Drôle de Drame*, the Carné-Prévert "Gothick" fantasy, begins to compare with it. This was the film in which Louis Jouvet played a Scottish bishop, Jean-Louis Barrault dived stark naked into a lily-pond, Françoise Rosay lodged at a Limehouse brothel, and Michel Simon bred carnivorous orchids. It explored that highest reach of farce and artifice, in which the actor takes his part seriously but mocks himself for playing it. It began with its tongue in its cheek, and you left with your tongue in yours. The same is true of *Kind Hearts*.

In the 1949 Edinburgh Festival Guinness returned to the sub-astral plane which he had deserted since *The Ascent of F.6*. He played Harcourt Reilly, the equivocal pontiff of T. S. Eliot's *The Cocktail Party*, and his performance, as befitted a play which denied fruition to all terrestrial relationships, was chill, suave and austere. In January, 1950, *The Cocktail Party* reopened in New York, where its instant success enabled Guinness to lay the foundations of an American reputation which is now large enough to allow several off-Broadway cinemas to keep their patrons happy all the year round by running seasonal "Guinness Festivals". Harcourt Reilly, like Fancourt Babberley in *Charley's Aunt*, seems to be one of those timeless, ageless parts which can be played by actors of all types. I can think of no other leading role, except Hamlet, which could have been filled by personalities as disparate as those of Rex Harrison, Henry Daniell, Hugh Sinclair and Guinness. The play ran in New York for 409 performances: Guinness left halfway through to make two films, *The Mudlark* and *Last Holiday*.

1951 was the year of his splendours and miseries: triumph alternated disconcertingly with disaster. In pictures he flourished. *The Lavender Hill Mob* found him bowler-hatted, with a weird gleam in his eye, as a clerk who robs the Bank of England of a van-load of bullion, a role which, relishing such words, he describes as "fubsy". His performance was a complete, though sinister, recreation of the little man in Strube's cartoons, but Guinness makes no artistic claims for the film, which he dismisses as a romp. His affiliation to Ealing Studios, continued in Alexander MacKendrick's *The Man in the White Suit*, is easy to explain. In Ealing pictures there is generally no hero in the accepted sense of the word, but only a whimsical hero-impersonator. The Ealing custom, embodied in films like *Whisky Galore* and *Passport to Pimlico*, is to hang its scripts on general themes, the most popular of which is the bizarre British, faced with yet another perfectly extraordinary situation. We see little of the boudoir, the *bagnio* or the American bar, but much of the police force, the civil service, and the small shopkeeper—strata of society to which Guinness is easily adaptable. In *The Man in the White Suit*, as a Cambridge graduate who invents a stainless, indestructible cloth and sees his brain-child strangled by industrial pressure, he resembled a waxen, poker-faced Chaplin; and the film, though it ended lamely with the disintegration of the cloth, had a considerable *succès d'estime*.

Henry Sherek, the ventripotent impresario who put on *The Cocktail Party*, had for some time been buttonholing his friends and informing them that Guinness was the best actor in the world; and in May, 1951, he backed his opinion to the hilt. Under Sherek's aegis, Guinness embarked on his Festival production of *Hamlet*. This was to have been his final deliverance from the spells cast on him by Gielgud and Guthrie, an affirmation that he existed in his own right, independent of counsel or rebuke. He cast the play himself, summoning a young B.B.C. producer, Frank Hauser, to collaborate on the direction. He also, to my perturbed amusement, invited me to make my first and only appearance on the professional stage as the Player King; and I am risking the charge of ingratitude, not to mention *Schadenfreude*, when I call the finished production a failure. But so (apart from a handful of politely intrigued reviews and one unaccountable *volte-face* on the part of the *Sunday Times*) it was. More precisely, it was a failure born of indecision, and fostered by the cancer of Guinness' humility. Unwilling, on the one hand, to work within the framework of tradition, he was fearful, on the other, of abandoning it entirely. This bred a fatal ambiguity, both in the production and his own performance.

Let him explain for himself, in the words of an article he contributed to *The Spectator* after the curtain had fallen on the 52nd and last performance. He began by saying that he had seen nine previous Hamlets, "of which that of Ernest Milton was undoubtedly the greatest"—a statement in which the dismissal of Gielgud and Olivier is already implicit. He continued: "When I came to play Hamlet for the first time, in 1938, in Guthrie's modern-dress production at the Old Vic, I was merely a pale shadow of Gielgud with some fustian Freudian trimmings, encouraged—he will forgive me, I know—by Guthrie. I list these things, as I believe they are important in the way of tradition and as showing how an actor can react against the traditional and yet be steeped in it and love it." The last sentence crystallises Guinness' dilemma. It brings to mind something Cyril Connolly once wrote of Chamfort, the aphorist. "His predicament," said Connolly, "is one with which we are all familiar . . . that of the revolutionary whose manners and way of life are attached to the old régime, whose ideals and loyalties belong to the new, and who by a kind of courageous exhibitionism is impelled to tell the truth about both. . . ." In *Hamlet* Guinness shunned both the old methods ("heroics, struttings and bellowings", he called them) and the new (Freudian, naturalistic, what you will). And having set up road-blocks on both the main highways, he lacked, as we shall see, the degree of self-confidence necessary to take the short-cuts he had originally mapped out for himself.

John Vickers

Hlestakov in *The Government Inspector*

Picture Post Libr

Herbert Pocket in the film of *Great Expectations*

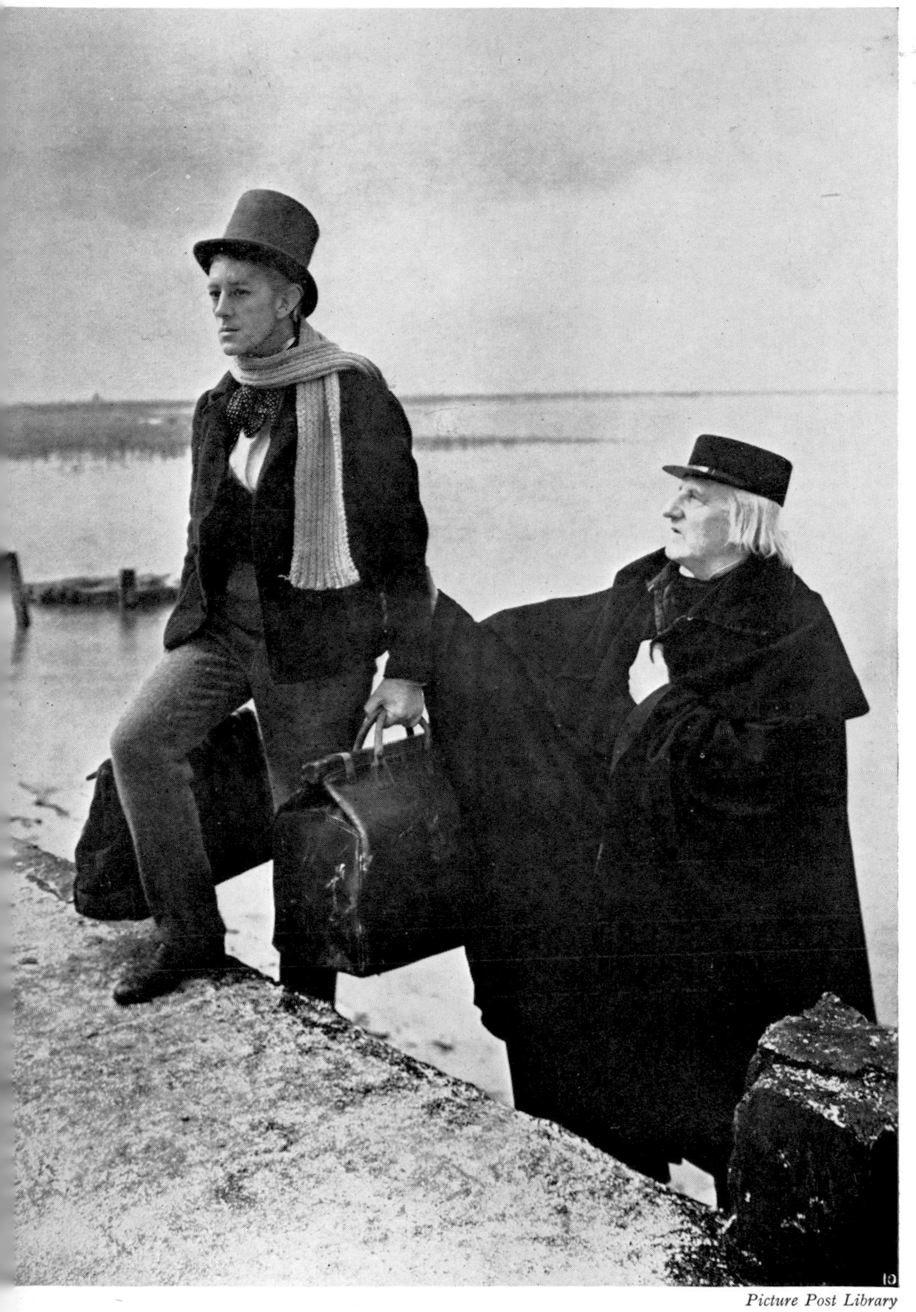

Picture Post Library

Great Expectations: with Finlay Currie

National Film Libr

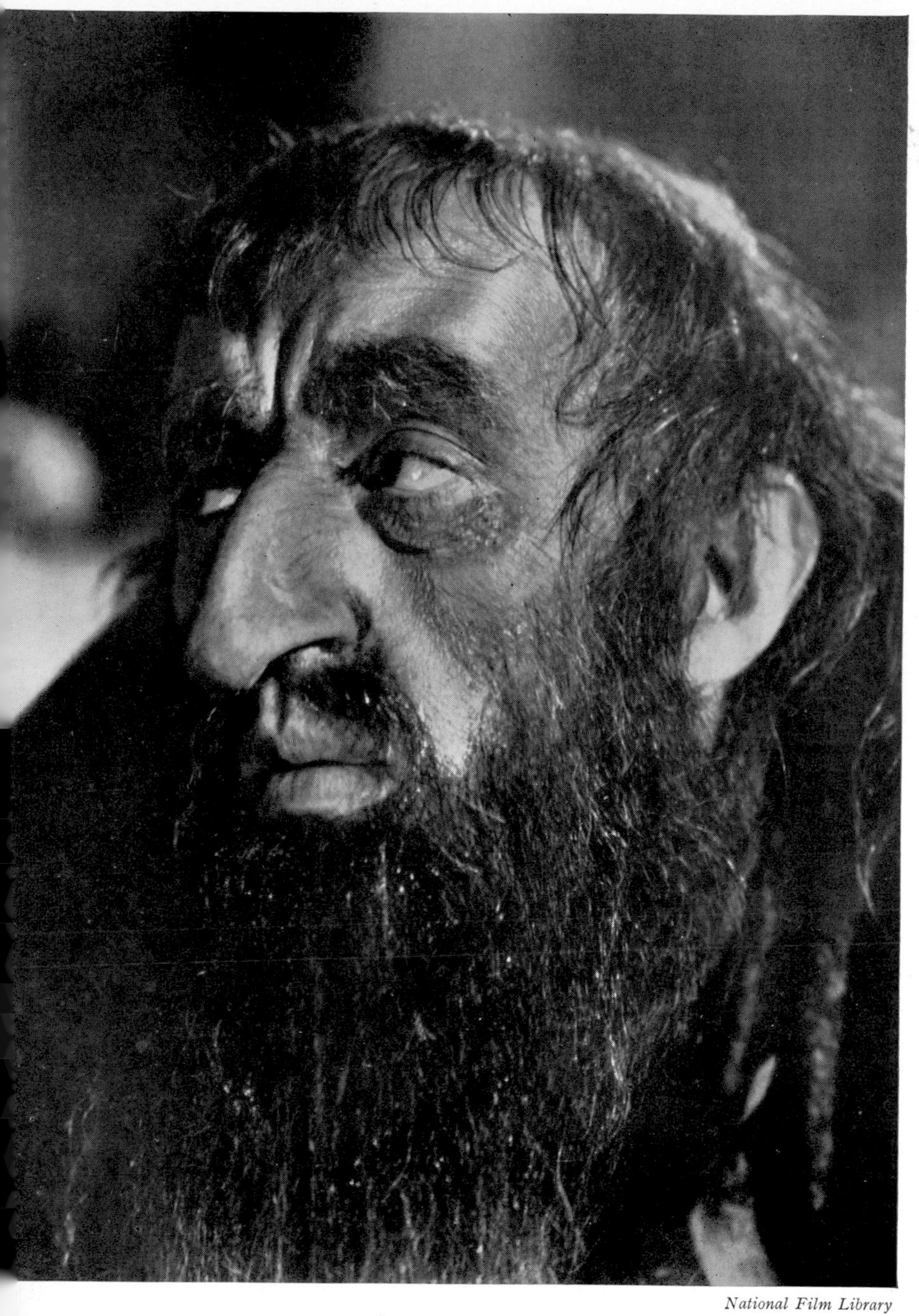

National Film Library

;in in the film *Oliver Twist*

Angus McB

Dr. James Simpson in *The Human Touch*

National Film Library

Six of Guinness' ten roles in the film *Kind Hearts and Coronets* (with Valerie Hobson, second from left)

Kind Hearts and Coronets Left: The Duke; Right: The Banker

"The only book on Shakespeare," his article goes on, "that opened windows on new horizons for me was Edward Armstrong's *Shakespeare's Imagination*—and that has nothing much to say about Hamlet. Granville-Barker I took gravely and steadily over a period of years, but he never fired me. When Madariaga appeared with his bombshell I was thrilled and appalled for a week, but came to the conclusion that I hardly agreed with a word he said. It was a challenging book, however, and from it sprang one aspect of my recent production. I was completely convinced by his assumption that the Elizabethan world was as much influenced by Spain as we are today by America." So a Spanish designer, Mariano Andreu, was engaged. Of the décor Guinness says: "It was partly the result of *reaction against* [my italics] permanent, semi-permanent and realistic sets in Shakespeare, and, above all, of a stubborn dislike of the rostrum. Rostrums, apart from cluttering the stage, tend to produce a one-foot-up, one-foot-down sort of acting which I find peculiarly dispiriting. I have very few conversations on the stairs in my own house, and see no good reason for making God's gift to an actor—a flat square stage—into something like the entrance to the Athenaeum." These are thoughtful opinions, with wit in their texture; but still the positive note is absent. Heaven forbid that Guinness should thunder in his own advocacy! But is there not something here of the highly intelligent, extremely self-conscious man who, thinking too precisely on th' event, refuses to commit himself for fear of exposing himself to ridicule? After all, if you react against permanent, semi-permanent and realistic sets, what is there left to support?

In the last part of his apologia Guinness says: "I followed Granville-Barker's advice and did not drop the curtain, as is usual, at the end of the 'Rogue and peasant slave' soliloquy. Now this seems to me to be the only daring, original and exciting thing we did in the whole production, and it escaped the critics' notice." In place of the customary thudding curtain, he points out, the audience got: " 'To be or not to be' within a minute and a half, followed by the 'nunnery' scene, followed by the social ease of 'Speak the speech'—in fact, they get the greater part of Hamlet's character stripped bare before them. . . . And all in the space of about fifteen minutes." Whether Guinness fully exploited this chance, I am dubious. That he could, in other circumstances, have done so, I am quite sure.

If I, an attenuated 24-year-old, was alarmed at the prospect of playing a robust and bearded tragedian, I was not alone in bafflement. Much of the casting was of an equally exuberant oddness. Guinness' intuitions about anything other than his own abilities are mostly unreliable, and he has a habit of attributing to other actors his own unique powers of self-transformation. Michael Gough, a charming, dour *jeune premier* of essentially modern style, was cast as Laertes; Walter Fitzgerald, whose glowering gruffness was all but untested in Shakespeare, played Claudius; and Gertrude was Lydia Sherwood, who, beyond a brief stay at Regent's Park in 1944, had not appeared in Shakespeare for about twenty years. A strange, plump newcomer named Ingrid Burke played Ophelia, and the Horatio (Robert Urquhart) had likewise had no previous Shakespearean experience. This *recherché* casting worked properly in only one performance, the busy and attentive Polonius of Alan Webb. Relentless direction might have extracted more from the players, and one sardonic comment might never have been made—that the production started out to be *fin-de-siècle* and finished up being end-of-term, with the headmaster's wife gallantly taking over Gertrude at short notice. But Guinness failed to act as a catalyst on the company. One noticed a curious deference in his conduct of rehearsals. Demurely, he would acquiesce in the suggestions of Frank Hauser, whom he had engaged as a sort of impartial censor—an error, because, as Hauser would readily admit, he was not ripe for the responsibility. In the early rehearsals some of Guinness' inventions were dazzling: about his Hamlet there was a touch of the headsman, judicious and inexorable, which excited us all. This was slowly ironed out. Guinness' reluctance to commit himself to solo direction worked its own downfall. Having cut himself adrift from safe Shakespearean tradition, he resigned the tiller and left the production becalmed. It was *Hamlet* with the pilot dropped.

A few traces of *echt* Guinness remained, but not the best.

His visual sense is not his strongest point, and it was at its most erratic in the climax of the play-scene, when he suddenly decided to indulge in a little expressionism. This took place just after I had taken leave of the Player Queen and dropped off to sleep. As the murderer crept up to slip me the potion, there was a slow black-out, except for a single spotlight on Claudius' face. Phosphorescent paint had been applied to the crown, the vial of poison and a great plastic left ear which I wore over my own: these glowed in the darkness, and the tableau as the poison was poured took on the aspect of an advertisement for a proprietary brand of rum. As an idea, provocative; but in execution, comic. It was cut out after the first performance. I remember handing the ear over to the stage manager and feeling, for a moment, remarkably like Van Gogh.

Guinness tells a disarming story about the events leading up to the fiasco of the opening night. He arrived at the New Theatre far too early, and killed time by strolling round the corner to the Garrick Club. After glancing at the newspapers, he was about to leave when his eye fell on the new bust of Forbes-Robertson, standing on its pedestal in the entrance hall. Ever a hostage to superstition, he looked about him and, seeing no one, reached up on tip-toe and touched Sir Johnston for luck. Duly consoled, he made for the door; and then noticed the bust of Irving. Warily, compulsively, he touched that too. These things going in threes, he thought he had better do the same for Shakespeare. The pedestal proved too high for him. Undeterred, he dragged up a heavy club chair, climbed on to the seat, and, wobbling, achieved his object. Having appeased the fates, he sauntered back to the theatre, where the fates quickly showed him what faithless harpies they are.

His generosity and loyalty to the cast both during and after the first night were beyond praise. At the end there were boos, to which he bowed gamely; and when the curtain fell for the last time, he turned to the rest of the company and said, very softly: "It was my fault. Don't blame yourselves. I gave up in the first act." Several powerful voices, among them Edith Sitwell's, pleaded the production's cause, but I do not think Guinness was much comforted. The blow to his pride had been shattering. But even when one has made the excuse that *Hamlet*, unlike most West End plays, opened without a preliminary tour or a *répétition générale*, it is still difficult to understand why no further rehearsals were called, after the first performance, to put things right. *Hamlet* was the first severe wound Guinness' career had received, and it was self-inflicted. New tissue was long in forming over it.

First he made a film, *The Card*, taken from Arnold Bennett's novel of the same name. This he chose partly in an effort to conquer the hitherto unresponsive provincial audiences (the hero is an East Midlander); partly because his role was that of an extrovert opportunist, a new departure for him; and partly because in it, for the first time since *Cousin Muriel* in 1940, he got the girl. His performance was full of cunning, a lively scamp with a crooked grin, but the film as a whole lacked substance.

His theatrical plans, meanwhile, had undergone a great deal of reshuffling and postponement. He had intended to follow *Hamlet* with *The Apple Cart*, playing Magnus; after which he had hopes of realising a life's ambition by appearing opposite Tallulah Bankhead and/or Edwige Feuillère. These gay and expansive projects now had to wait. In April, 1952, eleven months after *Hamlet*, he came back to the West End in *Under the Sycamore Tree*, a cautionary comedy by Sam and Bella Spewack, in which all the characters were ants—an ancient wheeze, last exploited by the brothers Capek in *The Insect Play*. Here, Guinness may have felt, was material he could swear to rise above. Ants are reputed to be full of formic acid, a few drops of which might with advantage have been injected into the wry, folksy philosophy of the play. To poke fun at the human race, the Spewacks poked an anthill, uncovering a brain-sick ant scientist who had learned enough about the ways of men to equip his fellow multipedes with speech and mechanisation, as well as enough D.D.T. to preserve the balance of power. Much of the wit was founded on variants of the line: "Six of my feet are killing me"; but there was an eery and memorable moment when the Queen of the Brown Ants sent over a Christmas card "with a photograph

J. Arthur Rank Organisation

National Film Library

Kind Hearts and Coronets Left: The Admiral; Right: The General

J. Arthur Rank Organisation

Kind Hearts and Coronets Left: The Suffragette; Right: The Parson

National Film Library

Left: Henry D'Ascoyne; Right: Ascoyne D'Ascoyne

National Film Librar

Whimple in the film *A Run For Your Money* (with Clive Morton)

National Film Library

George Bird in the film *Last Holiday* (with Beatrice Campbell)

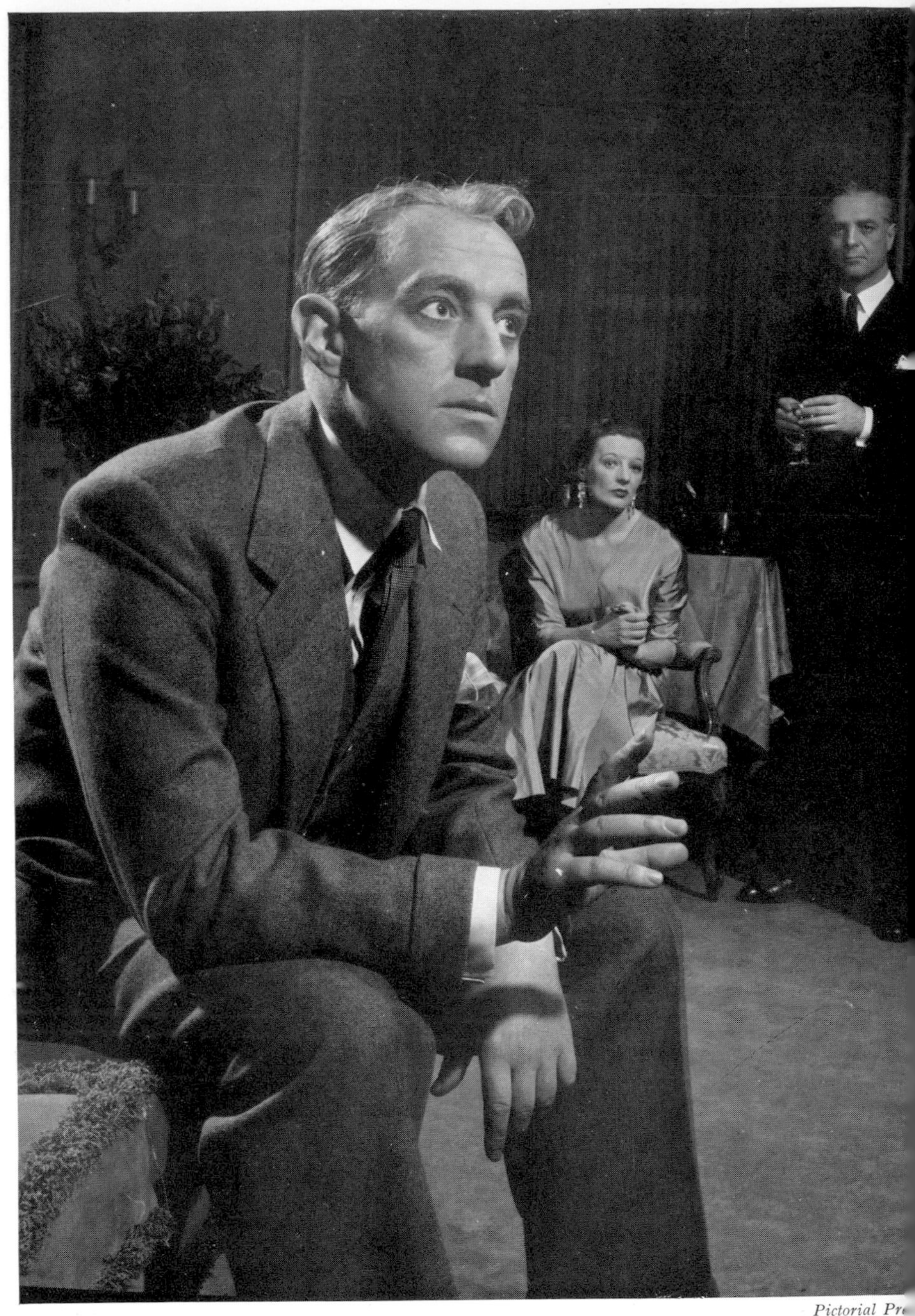

Pictorial Pr

Sir Henry Harcourt-Reilly in *The Cocktail Party* (Edinburgh and New York) with, in background, Eileen Peel and Robert Flemyng

Twentieth-Century Fox

Disraeli in the film *The Mudlark*

J. Arthur Rank Organisatio

Holland in the film *The Lavender Hill Mob*

J. Arthur Rank Organisation

Sidney in the film *The Man in the White Suit*

Houston Rogers

Hamlet (1951): The Duel Scene (with Michael Gough)

of herself at the mouth of her tunnel". The play was a jumble of unresolved revue sketches, all based on the neo-bestiary theme: entomologically it may have stood up, but logically it fell down. Guinness played the ant scientist with rubber-soled charm and mincing guile. He enjoys playing inventors, and he enjoys being several people—specifications amply covered by a role which required him to be doctor, engineer, psychiatrist, statesman, lover, nonagenarian and ant rolled into one. With head and eyes swivelling as if on ball-bearings, his whole performance was a long, sly, leisurely wink. Given a little more champagne in the dialogue, the result would have been a pure noggin of Black Velvet.

In 1953 he completed two pictures, both with Mediterranean backgrounds: *The Malta Story* and *The Captain's Paradise*. The B.B.C., with unusual perspicacity, then offered him the role of poor, defeated Winston Smith in a mooted television version of George Orwell's *1984*. He was much tempted: "I've never," he wrote, "appeared in bright blue in the Oxford Street stores"; but in the end he adhered to an earlier plan, which was to spend the summer in Canada, inaugurating a Shakespeare Festival at the township of Stratford-on-Avon, Ontario, where a quasi-Elizabethan arena theatre was being specially built. Here, physically remote from distractions of any kind, he played himself back into Shakespeare. With him went Guthrie, as director, and Irene Worth, his leading lady in the Edinburgh and New York productions of *The Cocktail Party*. Guinness came bowling down a ramp in a wheelchair as the fistulate King of France in a modern-dress version of *All's Well That Ends Well*, and then donned a fearsome mould-and-russet wig to play crookback Gloucester in *Richard III*.

There, at present, his career rests, and this interim report must, as far as facts are concerned, come to an end. What happens next? We can only speculate. One cannot forecast Guinness' future half as confidently as, having seen Gielgud's early performances, one could have predicted *his* probable line of development. For Guinness the choosing of a play is an all but insoluble problem: like most versatile actors, he is constantly being stymied by the discovery that nothing in the dramatic repertoire seems to have been written especially, distinctly, for him. Give him any part in the world, and he will be able to play most of it; but the parts he can play in their entirety, the parts which would use all of him, are not easily come by. In tragedy, perhaps, he might hit his full stride as one of Chapman's Jacobean *grands seigneurs*; as Byron, for example, in *The Conspiracy of Byron*, who says to his priest at shriving-time: "Leave my soul to me, whom it concerns." This ingrowing stoicism, this passion for spiritual privacy would chime well with Guinness' temperament. Or, in comedy, he might try the self-intoxicated Boswell of the *London Journal*, should someone pluck up courage and turn it into a play. If his private ambitions were fulfilled, he would play national heroes; Nelson, for one, then Gordon and Wolfe, and finally Captain Cook, whom he regards as the greatest Englishman, Shakespeare apart, who ever lived. It takes some effort to imagine him hardened to the mould of men like these, pioneers and commanders. How, with his ductile graces, should he convey their iron will? How simulate their stern, long-sighted gaze with his own, which always looks (though in fact it is not) a trifle myopic?

And anyway, to judge from his performances, he sympathises with the Lytton Strachey view of history, the lyrical-cynical view: surrounded by great events and grand designs, he can seldom keep an absolutely straight face. Whim, not will is his ruler. He is in many ways the most impetuous, least premeditated of actors. At one performance of *Hamlet*, stung by the unwonted brusqueness with which Rosencrantz delivered the line: "My Lord, you must tell us where the body is and go with us to the king", he obeyed instinct, strode the width of the stage, smiling glassily, and slapped the offender hard across the ear, almost knocking him into the orchestra pit. It was a purely automatic reaction. Afterwards, in the wings, he swarmed up to the bruised victim (who jumped nervously) and: "I'm so sorry," he said, his eyes moist with apology, "but you were so—so *insolent*, I felt I had to."

Were I to guide his future, I should probably begin by indicating that he can—and this is rare—act mind. He is one of the few people alive who could play a genius convincingly. How seldom one sees an actor, playing an author, whom it is possible to imagine constructing a coherent sentence, far less a masterpiece! Yet Guinness, I dare swear, would make a splendid Donne, and a more than tolerable Shakespeare, of whom he has already sketched a scenario for a film biography. Stendhal, Sterne, Catullus—these and dozens more would be within his range. After the men of letters, the wits. And then the murderers: one regrets that Chaplin has said the last cinematic word on Landru. My point is that the people Guinness plays best are all iceberg characters, nine-tenths concealed, whose fascination lies not in how they look but in how their minds work; people with secrets to hide from their fellowmen, people like poets and killers and saints, Clare and Crippen and Father Brown. Guinness can convey, by his voice and bearing, the existence of little fixed ideas, frisking about behind the deferential mask of normality. The parts he plays are, so to speak, injected hypodermically, not tattooed all over him: the latter is the star's way, and Guinness shrinks from it. The externals of acting are other men's business. Guinness is not and never will be a star in the sense that Olivier is. Olivier, you might say, ransacks the vaults of a part with blow-lamp, crowbar and gunpowder: he is the best of the Bill Sikeses. Guinness, on the other hand, is the nocturnal burglar, the humble Houdini who knows the combination and therefore makes no noise. He does everything by stealth. This technique is his patent, which in part explains why it will leave no descendants. He will illumine many a blind alley of subtlety, but blaze no trails. Like Buckingham in *Richard III*, he is "deep-revolving, witty": the clay image on whom, from within, the witches work. An innocence as of the womb makes his face placid even when he plays maniacs.

As an actor, then, he is introverted, and he is rapt: so, too, you may argue, was Irving. But his was an explosive raptness, which shook its fist at the gods. Guinness waves away awe with a witty fingertip, and deflects with a shrug the impending avalanche. His stage presence is quite without amplitude; and his face, except when, temporarily, make-up transfigures it, is a signless zero. The conclusion is inescapable: a big performance from him must concentrate on the interior, not the exterior of the character he is playing. His territory is the man within.

Hence, whether he likes it or not (and I suspect he does), his true métier will always be eccentrics—man reserved, blinkered, shut off from the rest of us; and, comically or tragically, obsessed. Within such minority men there is a hidden glee, an inward fantastical glow. Inside their souls, Guinness is at ease. Thankfully, in life as in plays, they are many. We can still be glad of nonconformity, and warm to the oddments, the outcasts and the loons. To watch Guinness playing them, and doing them as proud as only he can, is to recall Lamb's tribute to Munden, so often and so ineptly applied to other actors: "He is not one, but legion. Not so much a comedian, as a company. If his name could be multiplied like his countenance, it might fill a playbill. He, and he alone, literally *makes faces*. . ."

Along with his wife Merula, his son Matthew, two dogs, a Siamese cat and a grey parrot, Guinness lives in a spacious and stagnant Regency square near Hammersmith Bridge. Here I have seen him make many outlandish faces; describing, perhaps, a rehearsal mishap, maliciously observed and not for publication. "And so," he will cry, acting it out, "one came capering on, one pranced across the stage, with all *this* going on"—a wild waving of the arms—"and all of a sudden one felt terribly silly, because . . ." He pauses to cover his mouth and chuckle. The use of the impersonal third person is characteristic. It brings us back to where we started: to the persistent, ubiquitous anonymity of Alec Guinness.

The final judgment on him must remain undelivered for many seasons to come. There will always be those who smile, finding him quaint, and these will be his enemies; while on the other side, a much quieter throng, there will be those who stare, finding him unique. Garrick's lines on Goldsmith come, not irrelevantly, to mind:

> "Here, Hermes, says Jove, who with nectar was mellow,
> Go, fetch me some clay,—I will make an odd fellow . . .
> For the joy of each sex on the world I'll bestow it—
> This scholar, rake, Christian, dupe, gamester and poet!"

Guinness has been all of these for our pleasure, and this is not the end.

Houston Rogers

Hamlet: The Closet Scene (with Lydia Sherwood)

Houston Roger

Hamlet (1951): The Prayer Scene (with Walter Fitzgerald)

hotos: Angus McBean

Three Studies of the Ant Scientist in *Under the Sycamore Tree* (with Diana Churchill and Daphne Anderson)

News Chronic

Under the Sycamore Tree: The Ant Scientist in the last scene

J. Arthur Rank Organisation

"Denry" Machin in the film *The Card* (with George Devine)

J. Arthur Rank Organisati

"The Card"

J. Arthur Rank Organisation

Peter Ross in the film *Malta Story* (with Muriel Pavlow)

British Lic

Henry St. James in the film *The Captain's Paradise* (with Celia Johnson)

Canada Wide Photo

Richard III, at Stratford-on-Avon, Ontario

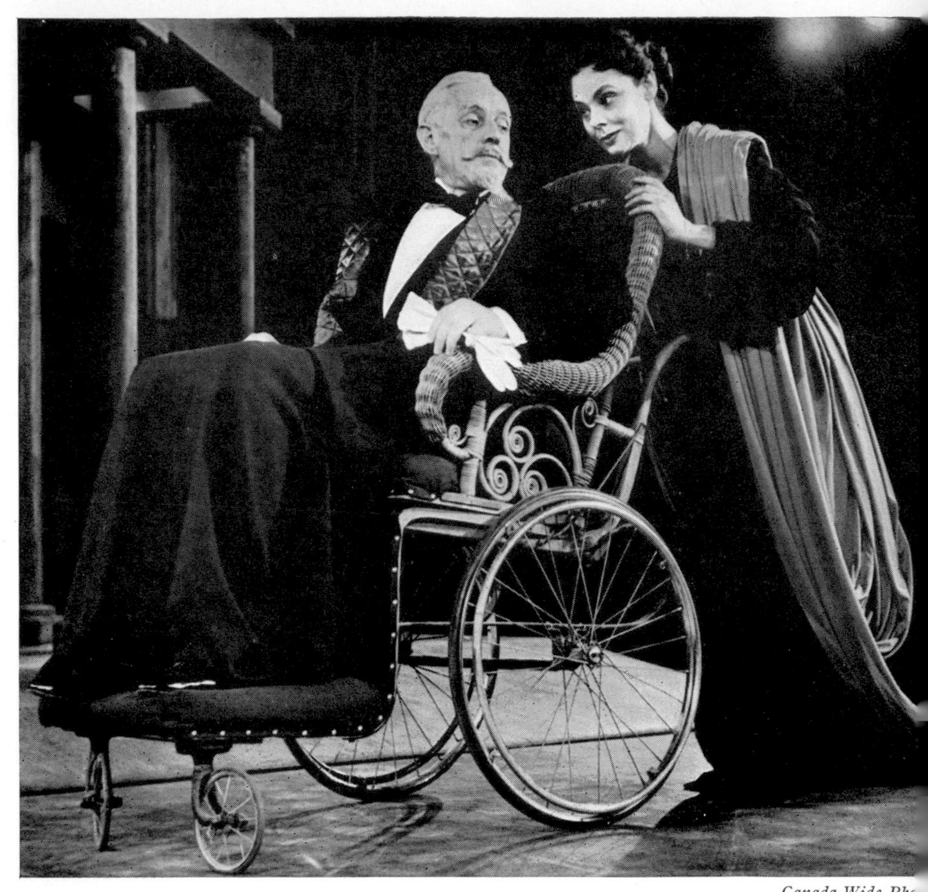

Canada Wide Pho

Stratford-on-Avon, Ontario: the King of France in *All's Well That Ends Well* (with Irene Worth as Helena)

CAREER OF ALEC GUINNESS

STAGE

1934

April — Non-speaking junior counsel in *Libel!* by Edward Wooll, Playhouse Theatre (Dir.: Leon M. Lion)

August — Three small parts in *Queer Cargo* by Noel Langley, Piccadilly Theatre (Dir.: Reginald Bach)

November — 1934–July 1936: With John Gielgud's Company, New Theatre:
Osric and Third Player in *Hamlet* (Dir.: John Gielgud)
Wolf in *Noah* by André Obey (Dir.: Michel Saint-Denis)
Sampson and Apothecary in *Romeo and Juliet* (Dir.: John Gielgud)
The Workman (and later Yakov) in *The Seagull* by Anton Tchehov (Dir.: Theodore Komisarjevsky)

September — 1936–April 1937: With the Old Vic:
Boyet in *Love's Labour's Lost* (Dir.: Tyrone Guthrie)
Le Beau and William in *As You Like It* (Dir.: Tyrone Guthrie)
Old Thorney in *The Witch of Edmonton* by William Rowley, Thomas Dekker and John Ford (Dir.: Michel Saint-Denis)
Reynaldo and Osric in *Hamlet* (Dir.: Tyrone Guthrie)
Aguecheek in *Twelfth Night* (Dir.: Tyrone Guthrie)
Exeter in *Henry V* (Dir.: Tyrone Guthrie)

1937

June — To Elsinore with the Old Vic:
Osric, Player Queen and Reynaldo in *Hamlet* (Dir.: Tyrone Guthrie)

September 1937–May 1938: With John Gielgud's Company at the Queen's:
Aumerle and the Groom in *Richard II* (Dir.: John Gielgud)
Snake in *The School for Scandal* by R. B. Sheridan (Dir.: Tyrone Guthrie)
Fedotik in *The Three Sisters* by Anton Tchehov (Dir.: Michel Saint-Denis)
Lorenzo in *The Merchant of Venice* (Dir.: John Gielgud)

1938
June — Louis Dubedat in *The Doctor's Dilemma* by George Bernard Shaw, Richmond Theatre (Dir.: Bernard Miles)

September–December: With the Old Vic:
Arthur Gower in *Trelawny of the "Wells"* by A. W. Pinero (Dir.: Tyrone Guthrie)
Hamlet in *Hamlet* (Dir.: Tyrone Guthrie)
Bob Acres in *The Rivals* by R. B. Sheridan (Dir.: Esme Church)

1939
January–April: Tour of Europe and Egypt with Old Vic:
Hamlet in *Hamlet* (Dir.: Tyrone Guthrie)
Chorus in *Henry V* (Dir.: Tyrone Guthrie)
Bob Acres in *The Rivals* (Dir.: Tyrone Guthrie)
Emile Flordon in *Libel!* (Dir.: Leon M. Lion)

June — Michael Ransom in *The Ascent of F. 6* by W. H. Auden and Christopher Isherwood, Old Vic (Dir.: Rupert Doone)

July — Romeo in *Romeo and Juliet*, Perth (Dir.: Willard Stoker)

December — Herbert Pocket in *Great Expectations*, adapted by Guinness from Dickens' novel, Rudolf Steiner Hall (Dir.: George Devine)

1940
March — Richard Meilhac in *Cousin Muriel* by Clemence Dane, Globe Theatre (Dir.: Norman Marshall)

May — Ferdinand in *The Tempest*, Old Vic (co-directed by George Devine and Marius Goring)

September-December — Toured England as Charleston in *Thunder Rock* by Robert Ardrey (Dir.: Herbert Marshall)

1941–45 — In Royal Navy. Guinness was released temporarily in December 1942 to play Flight-Lieutenant Graham in *Flare Path* by Terence Rattigan, Henry Miller Theatre, New York

1945

April — Nelson in *Hearts of Oak* Pageant, Albert Hall

1946

June — Mitya in *The Brothers Karamazov*, adapted by Guinness from Dostoevsky's novel, Lyric, Hammersmith (Dir.: Peter Brook)

July — Garcin in *Vicious Circle* (*Huis Clos*) by Jean-Paul Sartre, Arts Theatre (Dir.: Peter Brook)

September 1946–May 1947: With the Old Vic at the New Theatre:
The Fool in *King Lear* (Dir.: Laurence Olivier)
Eric Birling in *An Inspector Calls* by J. B. Priestley (Dir.: Basil Dean)
De Guiche in *Cyrano de Bergerac* by Edmond Rostand (Dir.: Tyrone Guthrie)
Abel Drugger in *The Alchemist* by Ben Jonson (Dir.: John Burrell)

September 1947–May 1948: With the Old Vic at the New Theatre:
Richard II in *Richard II* (Dir.: Ralph Richardson)
The Dauphin in *Saint Joan* by George Bernard Shaw (Dir.: John Burrell)
Hlestakov in *The Government Inspector* by Nicolai Gogol (Dir.: John Burrell)
Menenius Agrippa in *Coriolanus* (Dir.: E. Martin Browne)

1948

September — Directed *Twelfth Night* for the Old Vic at the New Theatre

1949

February	Dr. James Simpson in *The Human Touch* by J. Lee Thompson and Dudley Leslie, Savoy Theatre (Dir.: Peter Ashmore)
August	An Unidentified Guest (Sir Henry Harcourt Reilly) in *The Cocktail Party* by T. S. Eliot, Lyceum Theatre, Edinburgh (Dir.: E. Martin Browne)

1950

January	Repeated the role at the Henry Miller Theatre, New York

1951

May	Hamlet in *Hamlet* (co-directed by Guinness and Frank Hauser), New Theatre

1952

April	Ant Scientist in *Under the Sycamore Tree* by Sam and Bella Spewack, Aldwych Theatre (Dir.: Peter Glenville)
July–August	1953: At the Shakespeare Playhouse, Stratford-on-Avon, Ontario King of France in *All's Well That Ends Well* (Dir.: Tyrone Guthrie) Richard III in *Richard III* (Dir.: Tyrone Guthrie)

FILMS

1946	*Great Expectations* (Dir.: David Lean)
1948	*Oliver Twist* (Dir.: David Lean)
1949	*Kind Hearts and Coronets* (Dir.: Robert Hamer)
	A Run for Your Money (Dir.: Charles Frend)
1950	*Last Holiday* (Dir.: Henry Cass)
	The Mudlark (Dir.: Jean Negulesco)
1951	*The Lavender Hill Mob* (Dir.: Charles Crichton)
	The Man in the White Suit (Dir.: Alexander MacKendrick)
1952	*The Card* (Dir.: Ronald Neame)
1953	*Malta Story* (Dir.: Brian Desmond Hurst)
	The Captain's Paradise (Dir.: Anthony Kimmins)
	Father Brown (Dir.: Robert Hamer)